The Rock, his work is perfect,
for all his ways are justice.
Deuteronomy 32:4

Eight Miracles: A Memoir

The Archangel Gabriel is my
most precious caretaker.

BY MARY JO NIESON

EIGHT MIRACLES,
A MEMOIR

Psalm 19:14 "Let the words of my mouth and the meditation of my heart be acceptable in the sight, O Lord, my Rock and my redeemer."

by

Mary Jo Nieson

ISBN: 978-0-9995739-0-7

Published by

Detroit Ink Publishing

Detroit MI 48201 USA

Dedication

This book is dedicated to my daughter, to my many teachers, and to all those who may choose to read here.

Forward

As the years of my life have turned into decades, I have realized the many meaningful supernatural experiences I have had with the Divine. All of these have touched the deepest part of my heart. God has never left my side.

Some incidents were for my healing, others delivered for my protection or to raise my consciousness. Each one was given to me for and with love. All of them have brought my awareness closer to the spirit world.

I have been moved to chronicle these specific miracles to honor and thank God and His Dominion of His Son Jesus Christ, the Holy Ghost and His array of Angels for their obvious love and care.

My intent is also to encourage others for recognition of what otherwise might be thought of as imagination or odd coincidences. Answers to prayers can come in strange ways. God creates these moments just for us when we most need a light in the darkness. For me it was exhilarating and gave me encouragement to go on as I hope this small piece does for you, the reader.

Psalm 19:14: "Let the words of my mouth and the meditation of my heart be acceptable in the sight, O Lord, my Rock and my redeemer."

Prologue

I was raised an all-American girl during the 60's in Cleveland, Ohio by a working-class family. Ordinary by most standards, those days seemed so simple yet there was also an underlying conflict.

The major themes in my life were already present in my youth. A deep love and appreciation of the earth gleaned from my paternal grandparents; city dwellers who left generations of two farming families after WWII. I was geared for gardening, birdwatching, rock collecting, and the love of dogs and all animal life. I evolved into what I call an urban naturalist.

I left Ohio for Detroit, Michigan in the early 70's after my freshman year at Cleveland State University. I was able to transfer my position as a pharmacy assistant to the same drugstore chain and started my sophomore year at Wayne State University. This began my youthful, independent quest for love and the meaning of my life.

A few years later came marriage; induced by familial and societal pressure since we had been cohabitating. A month later my new husband sold my teal blue 1968 Chevrolet BelAir without my permission or knowledge. Since we lived miles outside of the city and he commandeered the other vehicle, I was left stranded.

Not long after the baby carriage arrived with my precious, lively, bright and beautiful baby girl. She will always remain the biggest treasure of my life.

By the time my little girl was two years old, I headed back to school part-time and I worked student jobs on campus to pay my tuition and to pay for day care. In the summer, I was a lifeguard on Belle Isle. During the last semester of my senior year, it became apparent I was to be stymied in my progress by my husband. This inevitably led to a contentious divorce with various forms of abuse perpetrated upon myself and later our daughter.

Free at last, I became a divorced single mother of the 80's continuing on my quest. My daughter and I grew up together in many ways under some tragic circumstances with a backdrop of emotional and psychological drama. I somehow managed to complete my B.A. in Anthropology and was immediately accepted into graduate school. Instead, I chose to move on to procure an associate degree in Computer and Data Processing to further improve my employment possibilities. In the midst of completing this coursework, an acquaintance told me about a union apprenticeship to become a steam power plant engineer.

The mere thought of four more years of study along with a full work week exhausted me, but I needed a more immediate and secure standard of living for my daughter and myself. I had no idea how steam became electricity but nonetheless applied for the apprenticeship. I made it through the five-part application process and to my great surprise was admitted to the first group. It turned out to be a blessing of not only abundance, but of knowledge.

Physics is the primary subject of understanding for a steam engineer, and I had never studied physics. Learning about absolute pressure in the universe, I finally learned the magic of my father's barometer and weather predictions! Between training for power plants and the science of cross cultural comparison in anthropology I felt I had a handle on what makes the world turn. I still had many surprises to come.

Midway into my career as a stationary engineer I met a co-worker who was a member of the Church of God in Christ. We became good friends and I was excited when she invited me to attend her church. Growing up my mother had referred to that church as Holy Rollers. It sounded so curious to me since I was raised a staid Episcopalian. It was certainly easier to stay awake in my friend's church but my childhood vision of all the parishioners rolling on church floors never materialized!

What did happen was a renewed interest in the Bible. I had read it through as a young girl, but the pastor's sermons gave me a new perspective as I began to review my life. I now felt my quest for the meaning of life and how I fit in might have an answer. Lo and behold what did I discover but quotes about the Rock! Suddenly I was a girl again hearing my name called from high in the trees.

1 SAMUEL 2:2: "There is none holy like the Lord there is none besides thee; there is no rock like our God."

Chapter 1: Finding the Rock

Cleveland, Ohio 1963: a momentous year for the nation who watched the assassination of our beloved president, John F. Kennedy, and a momentous year for me on both personal and spiritual fronts.

It was May, a lilting end-of-school year day, and there I was at the corner of my block, a ten-year-old fifth grader performing crossing guard duties, happily keeping my younger classmates safe from the residential drivers. Even today my nickname for myself is the 'Safety Girl' since I truly enjoy protecting others. When the day's duties were finished, it was necessary to return my yellow crossing flag and chest banner. I walked the block back to the K-6 school and returned towards home. Past the baseball backboard where later, walking home from Jr. High, I learned about kissing from the dark and handsome Freddy.

Back on my corner, I noticed how quiet it was for being right after school. I had walked only a few steps past the empty lot where we played baseball and football to reach the buckeye tree in my front yard. The heavily leafed maples above me suddenly called out my name. I spun to look to the rear, surely someone had run up behind me. No one. I looked up into the many fluttering leaves expecting to see that someone had climbed up there. I felt the late spring day warmth and the definite male voice called my name once more.

I ran home and straight to my bedroom. No one else was home but the dog and cat, yet I took no notice of them. I closed the door and lay breathless on the bed, which was next to the window facing the back door to my tiny private eagle's nest porch. I closed my eyes and like a dream I saw a huge rock in the distance. It seemed I anticipated it as it moved closer and closer to my bare feet. Almost as two opposing magnets my feet and the rock connected. I felt myself rise up, as if by like levitation. Unfortunately, that is all I recall, and I have no conscious memory of what happened next.

Later that same summer, lightning hit the chimney top next door. It was directly across from my bedroom window where my bed was located. There was only a narrow driveway's width between our homes. I awoke to a blinding flash and a scream mixed with the sound of bricks crashing and glass breaking. Thankfully the bricks and glass all fell through the kitchen window below my room. In the mind of the ten-year-old girl I was, it felt like God had just punctuated her supernatural Rock experience, impressing the message upon her young world. As an adult, I imagined I had been called up by a Divine spirit council dressed totally in white, a presence to remind me of my soul contract and to encourage me onward.

Growing up I loved to read, which opened up my small world to others' exciting adventures. By the time I was ten, I had the freedom to walk the two blocks alone to the library, which was a treat in itself. The librarian had given me permission to read books on one wall in the adult section of the library. During this same time period, I was also being prepared for confirmation into the Episcopal church. Our classes led me to read the Bible through. No doubt much of it went over my head, but my copy of the Bible had pictures too. I clearly recall often sitting on my bed cross-legged, staring at the picture of Jesus holding children and beckoning others with his outstretched hand. We've all heard, "Let the children come to me and do not hinder them." (Matthew 19:13) I wanted to know the love and protection he was offering those children.

Years later, I have learned about meditation and ways its peace can be achieved. Deep concentration on an object or thought and repetitive music are two ways and I have done both without knowing or purposely trying. It can be described as conscious dreaming.

When I was attending my friend's Church of God in Christ I never saw anyone rolling on the floor, but I found out that it was acceptable to move with the music or shout praises. I certainly heard some poignant sermons that seemed to speak directly to me. The sermons gave me a renewed interest in the Bible, so I began to study with pointers from the sermons that especially moved me. I cannot describe the elation and incredulous emotions I felt when I read in Isaiah that God is an everlasting Rock. My life took on new meaning as the Rock became real. I began to understand the loving support and grace God had given me throughout my life with the help of his angels. Especially the Archangel Gabriel, my most precious caretaker and guardian angel.

Deuteronomy 32:4 "The Rock, his work is perfect; for all his ways are justice."

Chapter 2: Finding A Guardian Angel

I have learned that guardian angels make themselves known to us during the best and worst moments in our lives. In addition, I understand that each one of us has our own guardian angel that stays with our spirit from incarnation to incarnation. The first time I became quite aware I might actually have a guardian angel was definitely one of those worst moments in life. It was in fact a possible life or death moment. Yet even then in that very moment I hesitated to respond to his booming bass voice.

I had a moonlighting job as the afternoon shift boiler operator in the power plant of a construction site. It was huge hospital building measuring 2.2 million square feet. A cement boiler room is very cold without any insulation, no heat stayed in the high ceiling space, and there were no real restrooms. Finally, mid-winter as construction progressed a creature comfort of a plywood bathroom with a locked door and even a sink for hand washing appeared four floors up in the center of the building site. It was very much worth the solo trek out of the perimeter set by the boiler room to the center of the site and up the stairs. All the workers were usually gone by 7 p.m. and the security guards made their rounds not long after, shutting down nonessential lighting.

I carried a flashlight and a short pipe length with a bushing on the end, a nod to a minor bit of protection. I always peeked out the commode door before I exited. Once I was met with a pair of eyes, I squealed a bit and ducked back in until I realized they hadn't been human! It was a cat who followed me all the way back to the boiler room and begged with her paws like a dog for my dinner. At the end of my shift she walked out and hopped into my car. Mercy Ann was a sweet calico I had for many years.

This night, seeing no one, I headed down the stairs to the basement level when I realized the guards had already been through and it was dark. I noted to myself what a target I presented in the dark hall with my flashlight passing open cubbies and doorways along the way. A building under construction is almost impossible to keep secure. I could see the well-lit pump room just ahead, so I scurried on and breathed a sigh of relief as I stepped inside. I only had to cross this room, turn right into the water treatment room and up the stairs to the main floor boiler room. Like a rodent, I turned to follow the wall. The compressors were on my right chugging rhythmically away as I gave them a passing check. I made a quick left to pass the rows of pumps, and suddenly I heard a bass male voice say, "Go to the center of the room!" Feeling confused since the voice was not outside of me, I took another step, only to hear again, "Go to the center of the room!!" this time the voice was a bit louder. Still unbelieving, I lifted my right foot and simultaneously heard loud and clear "I SAID GO TO THE CENTER OF THE ROOM NOW!!" Three times is the charm, and so I went to the center of the room between the rows of pumps. I began to thread my way forward, alert but oblivious to any real danger. The room was wide open.

Suddenly I saw movement to my right. There in the open storage cubby was a man trying to hide behind the wire spools. I stopped, I couldn't just walk away now. "I have seen you, now leave! This place isn't big enough for the both of us!" I declared. I had been warned there were thieves and homeless people hiding in parts of the building on occasion and here was proof. He began to approach me. I warned him off and out again, yet he continued towards me. I gripped my pipe and out of my mouth flew, "You won't be the first or last man I ever killed, now GET OUT!" He put up his hands in surrender and backed out the exit on the street side. Luckily the powerful cowgirl-speak worked, perhaps it had bubbled up from all the movie westerns my brothers and I used to watch as kids. As soon as he was out the door, I peeled off in the opposite direction to find the security guards.

Extremely grateful for the protection that night, I was glad to be going home to my teen daughter. Later, running the scene over again through my head I wondered how the right words to frighten the intruder off came so easily to me. I remembered reading somewhere in my Bible to not worry about what to say, as the Holy Spirit would put the words in our mouths when it was necessary. My Bible's Concordance showed me there are two places for this message, one being Luke 12:12.

At this point in time, I still had no idea who this angel was nor had I put together how often the angel had been present in my life. I had not realized that it was possibly always the same angel. Not even that it was most likely the same angel who called to me from the trees at age ten.

Mark 13:11 "...do not be anxious beforehand about what to say; but whatever is given you in that hour, say this, for you are not the ones speaking, but the holy spirit is."

Chapter 3: The Invisible Love Wrap

I awoke to my 5:30 AM alarm one typical early winter morning. I was awake before the sun had risen, yet I sat on the edge of my bed with my head in hands, so low in spirit and the day had yet to begin. I had recently returned to work after an on the job injury. I was out of personal time and was deemed fit for work. I was, however, still dealing with knee pain. A building engineer has a very physical job of operating and maintaining all heating, plumbing, and electrical systems. I was struggling daily with pain and the stress of trying to properly perform my work duties.

Suddenly I felt a warmth literally wrapped around me from behind, like a blanket; a blanket with emotion I could feel! An invisible love infused wrap like a mother bird wrapping wings of love around me. I was stunned, perfectly still as I absorbed the beauty of the love. It was over suddenly leaving me giddy and joyful; a complete turnaround.

"Who did that?" I asked myself out loud as I hopped around in excitement. A spirit of someone I know who passed on? An angel? No answer came, but it did feel like wings of love.

The important and lasting result for me this day was the knowledge that I was loved and cared for with enough depth of emotion for a spirit to act for me. My days were forever changed, and yet still, I did not realize this was my guardian angel.

Isaiah 26:4 "Is there any God but me? No, there is no other Rock; I know of none."

Chapter 4: Saving A Tooth

I grew up loving baseball. My father's family was big into baseball and football. I still remember Grandma running in from the kitchen in her apron to see what happened on Thanksgiving Day football games. I shared this love of sports with my daughter and I am so proud she became a pitcher for her high school fast pitch softball team. She went on to play in college and was also a College All Star.

After my daughter went away to college I found I had more free time to take on new activities. I started volunteering at the local humane society once a week and I also joined the coed slow pitch employee intramural team.

One game day while warming up, I was throwing catch with a male teammate. Each time I confidently watched the ball into my glove. WHAM! Something or someone bashed me in the mouth! That moment of darkness left me hunched over holding my mouth. There was blood on my hand, but I wasn't gushing. A teammate rushed over to check on me. She told me the ball had tailed off the heel of my glove and into my mouth. No more game for me, off to the dentist I went instead.

I walked into my dentist's office and luckily, he was there to see me. After he examined my mouth and teeth he told me that one of my front teeth had been damaged and it was dead. The tiny artery that feeds the tooth had been severed and the tooth was already turning gray. I needed serious repair work and was told to return the next day. I was extremely distressed at the thought of what had to be done. I have never felt comfortable in a dentist's chair, especially when local anesthetic is needed.

That evening I prepared soup for dinner as I could not chew and jarring the damaged tooth would cause considerable pain. Halfway through my meal, while delicately spooning the soup into my mouth, the unthinkable happened. As I pulled the spoon away, my hand stopped and rapped upwards directly on the damaged tooth, straight upward in one smooth motion that put me right through the ceiling! I began yowling and hopping around in deep pain. Yes, there was some cursing too. How could I do that to my tooth when I was being so careful, it seemed impossible I had done it!

Once I could breathe again, I went to the bathroom to check the tooth in the mirror. Despite the throbbing pain, the tooth appeared to be regaining color. I checked on it frequently during that evening and it truly was losing the gray color and turning white again. Now I realized this had been a good thing despite the pain!

The next day I was once again in the dentist's chair, and he could not contain his shock when he saw the tooth was no longer gray. He did his test for viability and the tooth was alive, no longer dead! He told me this with question marks in his eyes. He was having trouble believing his eyes and his instruments! He informed me this was an impossibility. The artery that supplies blood to the tooth is so tiny that usually once it is severed it can never flow again.

It truly had not been me who wielded the spoon like a healing tool! Once again, the angels brought their wings to my rescue!

PSALM 31:2 "Incline thy ear to me; rescue me speedily! Be a rock of refuge for me, a strong fortress to save me!"

Chapter 5: The Spiral of Life

My father was facing a decrescendo of life in his body. He would not be long in this world. A lifetime of smoking non-filtered cigarettes had taken a toll on his body and one organ was failing after another.

I had spent a week at his death bed and had to return home for work. Dad was never really conscious while I was there, but I felt he knew I was present. Before I left his side for the last time, I prayed over him for gentle passing. I felt he was waiting for me to leave.

It was a two-day drive from the Gulf Coast back to Michigan and I was halfway through my first day of solo travel. As I rounded a bend changing freeway directions I saw a lake to my right. Then an amazing kettle of turkey vultures came into view above the lake and trees. At least two hundred of the vultures formed a thrilling sight with their kettle spiraling upward black against the blue sky.

The sight triggered the memory of a recent time with my father on a fishing pier in Florida. Right behind his head a white cloud spiraled up into the sky. I had never previously seen a cloud such as this and asked Dad about it. He told me it was natural, that he saw them frequently there on the coast. I took a photograph of him with the spiral cloud.

Out of my reverie, I realized the spiral of vultures could well be a sign my father had passed over. I felt a loss, a weight lift. Within twenty minutes my cell rang; it was my mother. My father had indeed transitioned.

I was moved to tears of joy and sadness. My father's soul was free and he would finally know my truths.

2 Samuel 22:2 "The Lord is my Rock, and my fortress, and my deliverer."

Chapter 6: An Angel Cloud Trumpets

I was still living in Detroit on the far west side; a lot of crime due to prostitution and drugs was creeping into my area. I sometimes felt insecure on a jog even with a dog by my side. There was a small state park within driving distance that had lovely trails. I would often take my jogging partner, a hound mix, to run there. We both enjoyed the scents, sights, and sounds of more natural surroundings compared to cement and traffic lights. Once we almost ran smack into a small buck as we rounded a curve. My dog strained at the leash as I stood wide-eyed watching the deer bounce away from us.

On one of our trips, I exited the freeway ramp and headed west to the park. The sky watcher that I am noticed something unusual in the western sky. The clouds had made a huge formation that appeared as an angel blowing a trumpet. A complete heralding angel filled the western sky. I couldn't take my eyes off it the last few miles to the park. The angel was holding the trumpet with its hanging banner so that I almost heard it sound. I felt perhaps he was announcing something about the new millennium. Why else would an angel appear so clearly in the sky in front of me? I wondered if others besides myself on the road noticed it. I even looked around at the next light to see if others were looking at the western sky.

Once we entered the park, I could no longer see much of the sky due to the trees. I headed out to a place on the path where I had been moved to pray for the earth each time I would visit. Seeing the angel cloud beforehand encouraged me to continue that prayer time on each visit to the park.

Years later I learned that it is the Archangel Gabriel who always appears with his trumpet. He is also known as God's messenger, having brought joyful news to many in the Bible including the birth of Jesus to Mary. I decided the vision of Archangel Gabriel in the form of a cloud was not a random occurrence. It was years later that I finally came to realize the announcement he sounded that day was that he is my guardian angel.

LUKE 1:19 "I am Gabriel, who stands in the presence of God and I was sent to speak to you, and to bring you this good news."

Chapter 7: A Cardinal Miracle

I loved my paternal grandparents very much and was so lucky to have spent time with them as a child. They were the first generation in their families to leave the farm and make a life in the city in the 1920's. Grandpa sold Buicks and Grandma worked in a grinding wheel factory after my father and uncle graduated from high school. They shared their love of the natural world with me. I remember as a young girl standing in awe of their beautiful flower and vegetable gardens; not to mention the grape pies Grandma made from the arbor growing just outside her back door.

At age seven I found the magic; I was hooked when my first seed sprouted from the earth. My grade school had summer garden kits and a teacher would visit monthly to grade them. In September when we returned to school there was a garden fair in the auditorium for our produce. The entire school attended, and ribbons were given to the students for winning products.

Birdwatching is another connection to the natural world shared with me through my paternal family side. My father knew and could identify many birds and their calls. He would always share this with us kids when the opportunity presented itself, whether camping or in the backyard. I still keep my field glasses and book handy.

Cardinals have always been a favorite bird for me. So red, bright, and talkative, yet elusive. I have a memory of a cardinal, my grandfather, and my four-year-old self. We were near the garden by the rickety old garage on the alley. Grandpa hushed me, kneeled down, and held me close as he whistled back and forth with the bird. He urged me to try but I failed, of course. Grandpa smiled at my efforts and told me not to worry, I could always talk to the cardinal this way.

Fast forward to the 21st Century; I do whistle with the cardinals as they visit frequently, though I grow tired long before they do!

I sometimes care for a neighbor's dog. One time as I approached the neighbor's home, I saw a male cardinal sitting on the floor of the porch looking at me. I slowed my approach, expecting him to fly off. He didn't, and I moved closer, stopping with just three feet between us. I wondered if he was ill or injured, he was breathing very heavily. I stooped down and moved closer, but he stayed put. Although concerned the dog might harm him, I moved closer still and he looked directly at me and actually allowed me to pick him up.

Such a moving experience from such a skittish bird! The softness of his feathered body was indescribable. Within seconds he fluttered his silky self off into a nearby bush. I immediately connected with my grandfather's memory. I thought perhaps it could have been his birthday, but it turned out to be even more momentous. It was fifty years to the day of his death. I was seven years old that year too, and I remember it all so clearly. Grandpa's passing was a big loss to me and I insisted on seeing him in the casket at church to be sure he wasn't alive.

I grew up feeling like an outsider with my peers and family. Ultimately my self-confidence waned. In Earth Medicine the cardinal represents self-importance. Knowing my grandfather brought me a message fifty years later helped me to continue to rebuild my self-confidence. The cardinals and their calls are even more special to me now. I am loved and my grandparents are near.

Isaiah 44:8 "Is there any God but me? No, there is no other Rock; I know of none."

Chapter 8: A Prayer Answered

I grew up an active and agile girl. Having two younger brothers provided me with plenty of fun playing sports, biking and climbing trees. There were not, however, female sporting teams in the school system. Although the track coach in high school consented to me practicing with the boys' track team, he made it very clear I could not compete. It mattered not to me, I just loved running.

After my daughter's birth I was out of shape and overweight. I have always enjoyed feeling fit, but I also enjoy eating! At the time of my baby's first spring, I decided to begin jogging, and I have never stopped; it became a thirty-year habit. Never running, not racing, only jogging. Eventually it became my meditation time and I especially enjoy having a running dog to join me. There have been a few doggy running partners over time.

After I retired from my 25-year Stationary Engineer career and began my dog service business, I caught a bug. Being generally healthy, I consider a virus to be what I call an immune system download. I was just coming around from that bug, the day my dog fell off the porch, missing the steps as he launched for a squirrel. He had been an abandonment cruelty rescue puppy from my volunteer days at the humane society. He was not strong on his legs as a puppy, so we gave him plenty of walking therapy. He was never able to manage even long walks, but he got around just fine until that day. His spine was just weak enough at just over ten years old that the fall did him in. By the second day he made it clear he wasn't staying. The veterinarian brought him peace through euthanasia as I whispered in his ear we would meet again.

Then I relapsed, lying feverish and barely able to move, much like my dog on his last day. This went on for weeks and I lost my strength. I finally recovered enough to work and carry on, but jogging was no longer in the picture.

Over time I began to regain my strength, but it took a few years to slowly rehab my body. During this time, I had four dogs, and they too helped to build my stamina as I kept up my prayer of gratefulness for my present health and about the desire to return to jogging.

Finally, I was able to perform the RAF (Royal Air Force) fitness program. I had read that the actress Helen Mirren used this program to prepare for gym workouts. She's a bit older than me so I decided to give it a try and it was a great success. Another year passed with my strength waxing and waning over and over as I added in free weights and found an excellent chiropractor.

Suddenly I hit a consistency and decided in good spring weather to attempt jogging again. It was now or never in my mind as I was in my sixth decade of life. I headed for the park with the eldest dog, who was eleven years of age, he out did me! I didn't think my legs would hold me as the dog ran at the end of his leash. Never a fast or distance runner, I walked and jogged the dirt path.

Stretching and gasping for breath after the short quarter mile, I walked home. I kept at this regimen once a week and by week twelve I had built up enough endurance that I no longer had to stop to gasp for air. As I headed out the first day in my fourth month of training, it was a lovely summer day. I felt my form and gait returning as I jogged effortlessly. As I was rejoicing with laughter I heard a voice say, "There is your blessing." I was surprised, grateful, and excited enough to shed a tear as I thanked God for allowing me to return once again to my favorite activity.

Jogging with my dog is more than exercise to me. To run in nature with my dog allows me to be fully grounded on Mother Earth. In itself the meditation becomes a prayer for her bounty and beauty. I'm left feeling refreshed physically and mentally as my mind is freed while my feet touch the sweet earth and my dog joins in my pace.

1 Corinthians 10:4 "and they all drank the same supernatural drink. For they drank from the supernatural Rock which followed them, and the Rock was Christ."

AFTERTHOUGHTS

Certainly, my many prayers directed to the Almighty resulted in me receiving the angelic help of his winged minions. Even so, until the recent past, I mistakenly considered my Divine experiences to be random.

At some point, I realized I wasn't just lucky, and that there are no coincidences in life. I had enough supernatural experiences to send the curious me to seek out answers. My quest for love, the meaning of my life, and life in general has not ended. I am a student of life. This is our reason for being. Mother Earth is here in the 3rd Dimension for us to live her experience.

Even while writing this memoir I continued to learn about the angelic realm. Putting these memories on paper required me to review and be sure of the truth; even as my truth may not be another's. There are many perspectives when it comes to spirituality and religions. My story is told from a Judeo-Christian perspective. That is how it happened, and I did not arrange this, at least not in this embodiment. Divine communication came through a channel I had been taught and could understand. Angels are not exclusive to Christianity, they are celestial messengers known in virtually every religion.

I love it that God Himself created our diversity at the Tower of Babel. By doing so he gave us new ways to see and live on the hoop of Mother Earth. We are all part of the whole and together we are dependent upon her for life. We can come together in love and share our ways for enhancement of life.

God, Jehovah, the Great Spirit, Allah, Yahweh, these are a few of the names cultures use for the Divine Almighty. The One thing that never changes is the Rock Himself.

Synergy

Managing coincidences,
Finding meaning in déjà vu.
All in a day's work for a mystic
Pondering this cosmic glue.

Getting my mind so sticky,
Glad it all dries clear.
Synergy seems to call my name,
The question is, will I hear?

SUGGESTED READINGS

The Holy Bible, verses here from Revised Standard
Version, Cleveland and New York: World
Publishing Co., 1962

Akers, Ann Caroline, People of the Light: A
Lightworkers Path to Self-Realization, Victoria
B.C., Canada: Trafford Publishing

Bishop, Karen, Stepping into the New Reality,
USA: Booklocker.com Inc., 2008

Ghostwolf, Robert, Last Cry Native American
Prophecies Tales of the End Times Spokane, WA.:
Mystic House Publishing, 1993

Paramahansa Yogananda, Autobiography of a
Yogi, Los Angeles, CA: Self-Realization
Fellowship Publishers, 1971

Raven, Hazel, Angel Experience, London,
England: Bounty Books division of Octopus
Publishing Group Ltd., 2014

Schneider and Pieroth, Archangels and
Earthangels, Twin Lakes, WI.: Arcana Publishing,
2000

Villoldo PhD., Alberto, The Four Insights,
Wisdom, Power, and Grace of the Earthkeepers,
USA: Hay House, Inc., 2006

About the Author

Mary Jo Nieson presently has a private practice as a Certified Pet Massage Practitioner (CPMP) and is a member of the IAAMB/ACWT (International Association of Animal Massage and Body Work/Association of Canine Water Therapy.) She also offers holistic dog grooming in her Studio using organic products. Her recent writings have been about dogs, our relationships with them, as well as their care and health. She has been published in the former online journal Cosozo Living, and also in the local print Body Mind and Spirit Guide Magazine. She trained to write during a college bound curriculum in high school which allowed her to easily write term papers and she had a short stint as a journalist for the South End, the student paper for Wayne State University.

Ms. Nieson graduated from Wayne State University in 1981 with a Bachelor's Degree in anthropology. Her original interest in that field was the archaeology and history of Native Americans and the Egyptians that began as a young girl. As she continued her studies in this discipline, her interest morphed further into the cultural subfields of religion, language and medicine. The science of cross-cultural comparisons proved powerful for her naturally curious and open-minded character.

The role of leadership came easily to her after growing up the eldest of three children. Taking on a non-traditional career in steam power plant engineering after earning her B.A. took courage and fortitude but she was a single parent ambitious to be successful in life for herself and her daughter. She spent 23 years in that career before she left to serve dogs who have brought her joy and help her to stay grounded. She has lived all of her adult life in Detroit proper or the metro-Detroit area after relocating there a few short years after the 1967 uprisings. These days she can be found caring for her canine clients, spending time with her cats and dogs, or in her garden where she proudly eschews all pesticides and herbicides.